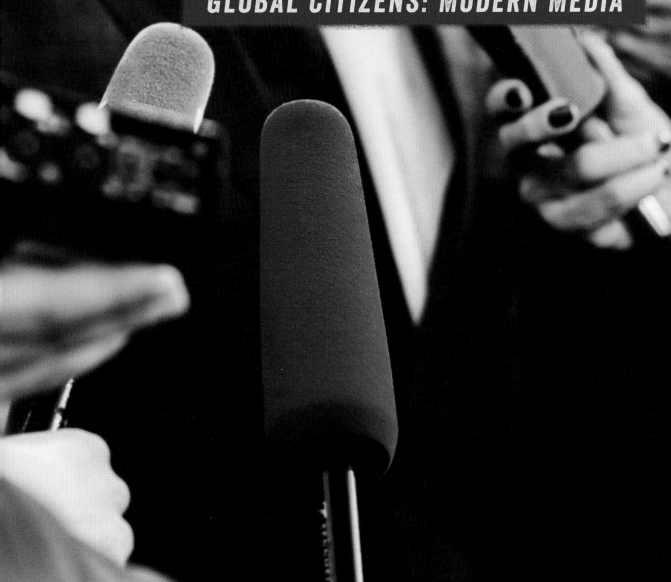

POLITICS AND THE MEDIA

GLOBAL CITIZENS: MODERN MEDIA

Published in the United States of America by Cherry Lake Publishing
Ann Arbor, Michigan
www.cherrylakepublishing.com

Content Adviser: Jessica Haag, MA, Communication and Media Studies
Reading Adviser: Cecilia Minden, PhD, Literacy expert and children's author

Photo Credits: ©Microgen/Shutterstock.com, Cover, 1; Title page of the *Relation aller Fürnemmen und gedenckwürdigen Historien* from 1609/University library of Heidelberg, Germany/Wikimedia Commons, 5; ©Romaset/Shutterstock.com, 6; ©goran cakmazovic/Shutterstock.com, 7; L'Illustration, Journal Universel (1848-9 volume)/Public Domain/Wikimedia Commons, 8; ©Everett Historical/Shutterstock.com, 9; ©mark reinstein/Shutterstock.com, 10; ©Pressmaster/Shutterstock.com, 13; ©GaudiLab/Shutterstock.com, 14; ©Photographee.eu/Shutterstock.com, 15; ©Niyazz/Shutterstock.com, 16; ©BlurryMe/Shutterstock.com, 19; ©antb/Shutterstock.com, 20; ©Stephen Coburn/Shutterstock.com, 21; ©Roman Samborskyi/Shutterstock.com, 22; ©amadeustx/Shutterstock.com, 25; ©stock_photo_world/Shutterstock.com, 26; ©Evan Meyer/Shutterstock.com, 27; ©chainarong06/Shutterstock.com, 28

Library of Congress Cataloging-in-Publication Data

Names: Mara, Wil, author.
Title: Politics and the media / by Wil Mara.
Description: Ann Arbor, Mich. : Cherry Lake Publishing, 2018. | Series: Global citizens. Modern media | Includes bibliographical references and index. | Audience: Grade 4 to 6.
Identifiers: LCCN 2018005239 | ISBN 9781534129290 (hardcover) | ISBN 9781534132498 (pbk.) | ISBN 9781534130999 (pdf) | ISBN 9781534134195 (hosted ebook)
Subjects: LCSH: Mass media—Political aspects—Juvenile literature. | Press and politics—Juvenile literature.
Classification: LCC P95.8 .M367 2018 | DDC 302.23—dc23
LC record available at https://lccn.loc.gov/2018005239

Cherry Lake Publishing would like to acknowledge the work of the Partnership for 21st Century Learning. Please visit *www.p21.org* for more information.

Printed in the United States of America
Corporate Graphics

ABOUT THE AUTHOR

Wil Mara has been an author for over 30 years and has written more than 100 educational titles for children. His books have been translated into more than a dozen languages and won numerous awards. He also sits on the executive committee for the New Jersey affiliate of the United States Library of Congress. You can find out more about Wil and his work at www.wilmara.com.

TABLE OF CONTENTS

CHAPTER 1

History: Politics and the Media

People have been communicating with each other for thousands of years. What began as rock carvings has slowly changed into books, newspapers, magazines, movies, radio, TV, and the Internet. Together, they are called **media**.

Common topics covered in the media are **politics** and politicians. Politicians work to further the interests of the people they represent. The media helps politicians get their message out in a way that the public can understand. Because the media is the main source people go to for political information, it has the

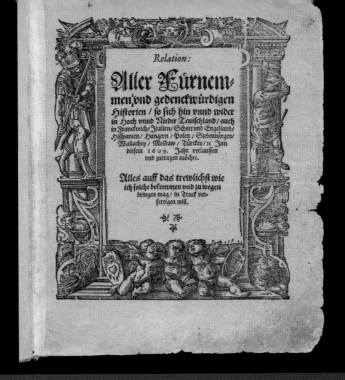

The world's first newspaper was published by Johann Carolus in 1605.

ability to sway public opinion. As a result, the relationship between politicians and the media has been both mutually helpful and unhelpful.

Earliest Times

Ever since humans started communicating with each other in large numbers, there have been both positive and negative reports about political leaders. Because of this, politicians have learned to use the media to their advantage.

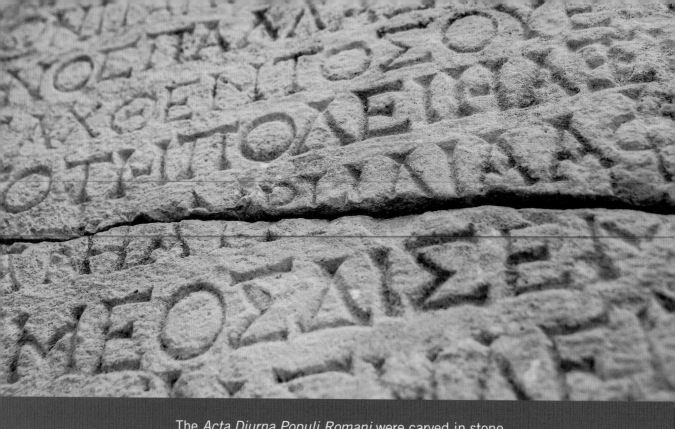

The *Acta Diurna Populi Romani* were carved in stone.

In ancient Rome, there was a popular document called *Acta Diurna Populi Romani*, or "Daily Acts of the Roman People." It was put in public areas where people could read it. It covered everything from local marriages to obituaries to funny stories. But in the beginning, it started as a way for Julius Caesar to brag about the achievements of his government. This helped increase support for him while destroying the efforts of his political enemies.

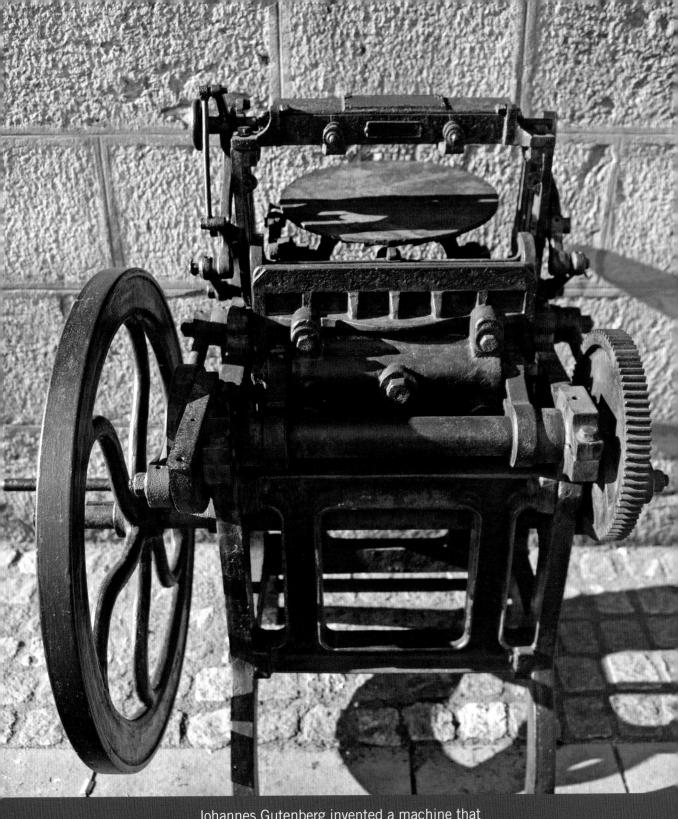

Johannes Gutenberg invented a machine that was able to mass produce books and newspapers.

Some claim that the newspaper we see and read today was a European invention.

Lack of Freedom

The **printing press** was invented in the mid-1400s. Ever since then, **journalists** have been eager to spread news about the mistakes and triumphs of elected officials. In the late 1690s, Benjamin Harris began printing the first newspaper in the North American colonies. But *Publick Occurrences, Both Foreign and Domestick* didn't get past the first issue. Great Britain's government had to first approve it—which it didn't. The government was afraid of the paper's influence on the public. The publisher

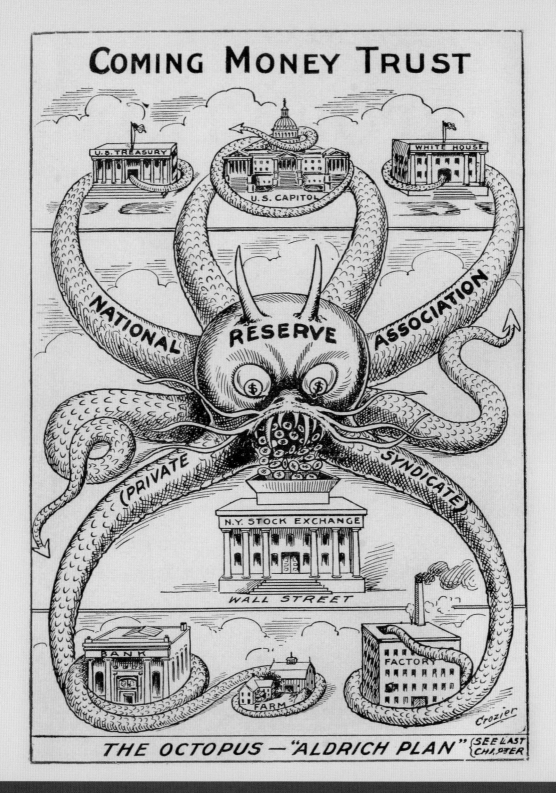

Political cartoons in newspapers were common in the late 1700s.
They are still common today.

Former president Richard Nixon is remembered as one of the most controversial presidents in U.S. history.

couldn't fight back. There was no United States of America yet. This meant there was no U.S. Constitution with its First Amendment that protected **free speech** and the freedom of the press. These rights weren't protected until the late 1700s.

The Era of Hostility and Mistrust

During the Vietnam War (1955–1975), there was a steep decline in the relationship between politicians and the media. It started with former president Lyndon B. Johnson's **administration**.

Johnson purposely misled the media about the war. He thought he was protecting the public. Instead, he caused mistrust among the media, public, and future administrations. Richard Nixon, the president after Johnson, deepened this distrust. He rarely spoke to reporters, and when he did, he was hostile.

Prior to Johnson's and Nixon's presidencies, the media held back on reporting negative news. This helped journalists gain a president's cooperation. But ever since this period in history, journalists have reported both favorable and unfavorable news about an administration. This trend has led politicians to be more guarded when speaking to the media.

Developing Questions

The relationship today between the media and many politicians is complicated by resentment and mistrust. What can be done to overcome these difficulties? What could each side do to improve the relationship?

CHAPTER 2

Geography: Political Media Around the World

Political reporting is always likely to stir up strong feelings among the public. In some countries, these feelings will be stronger. There are varying reasons for this, including the degree of **polarization** in politics and political **bias** in the media.

The Polarization Effect

When it comes to politics, most people have opinions about what is right and wrong. In some countries, the media deepens these opposing views, which creates more division.

In 2017, it was reported that both the U.S. political parties and the media coverage are the most polarized among Western

There are many different political parties across the world.

countries. Only 20 percent of **conservative** Americans trust the media, while 51 percent of **liberal** Americans do. Americans also feel that most of the major U.S. news outlets tend to be either very conservative or very liberal, with no real middle ground.

This wide gap between political parties and news coverage used to be unique to the United States. However, this growing trend is becoming the norm in Europe. In the past, many of its top news sources used to report more in the middle and attracted both conservative and liberal audiences. Today, that landscape

Not all countries have the same journalistic freedom as the United States.

has changed. In a 2017 survey, only 24 percent of British citizens said they trusted the news. This is a 12 percent drop in trust from just two years earlier!

Journalistic Freedom

According to Reporters Without Borders, the governments that allow their journalists the greatest amount of freedom include Norway, Sweden, Finland, and Denmark. The countries that restrict their journalists include North Korea, Syria, China, and the Sudan. Journalists in those countries are regularly fined or jailed if they report something the government doesn't like.

Sometimes journalists from around the world work together on a political story.

According to a survey, 67 percent of citizens in Venezuela believe the press has very little freedom to report the news.

Political Bias

The high level of polarization among Americans could be partially blamed on political bias in the media. The same now holds true for France, Germany, and Sweden. They believe, as Americans do, that their media coverage is more liberal. In contrast, Finland and Britain feel their news sources lean too conservatively.

Another problem in the media is the phenomenon of **groupthink**. Some say political bias and groupthink might have been the reason why journalists covered a big issue in 2016 the same way. Journalists covering President Donald Trump's campaign never expected Trump to win. Their articles reflected this view. It's easy for groupthink to happen when journalists are around others who share the same political views. And the majority of the country's **mainstream news** outlets are located in liberal areas, like New York City, Los Angeles, and Washington, D.C. But others argue that **fake news** and the rise of the Internet may be more to blame.

Gathering and Evaluating Sources

Media organizations in certain countries have a better relationship with the government and its citizens than others. Using both the Internet and your local library, determine which countries have the best media-government relations and which do not. Does the relationship between a country's news media and government mirror the citizens' relationship with the media and government? Use the evidence you find to support your argument.

CHAPTER 3

Civics: Politics, Media, and People

The average person relies on the media to inform them on important political issues. In an ideal world, political reporting would be **objective** and unbiased. It would not influence voters to think a certain way.

Just the Facts, Please

The best way to make good decisions as a voter is to find information about political matters that isn't filled with opinions. A survey conducted in 2017 found that 75 percent of citizens across

Some experts believe that journalists should listen more
and talk less—at least on social media.

A study found that people who trust the media are more likely to be satisfied with how their government is functioning.

Most people in the United States believe that the media
is a vital component to democracy.

38 countries want their political news to be unbiased. They believe
news outlets should not show a preference for one candidate over
another. In spite of this, only about 52 percent of those surveyed
felt journalists reported political news fairly. In the United States,
this percentage is lower. Only 47 percent of Americans believe
their media reports political news without bias. But reporting the
news with zero bias might not be possible. Journalists do their best
to decide what information is important to a story. Many in the
profession believe that journalists should seek to report "balanced"
news rather than the unattainable "unbiased" news.

Most U.S. citizens believe the news media is critical in informing people about public affairs.

The Media and the Political Process

In the past, Americans believed that media coverage improved the political process. They believed that elected officials feared being negatively portrayed and would act in the public's best interest. Today, people have less faith in the media's effect on politicians.

In 1985, about 65 percent of conservatives and 70 percent of liberals believed media coverage acted as a kind of **watchdog** over the behavior of government officials. At the start of 2000, those numbers were about even, at 60 percent for both conservatives and liberals. In 2017, however, the numbers were far apart. A study revealed that 89 percent of liberals believed the media helped keep the government honest. Only 42 percent of conservatives believed that. This suggests that conservatives had lost faith in the government and in the media, while liberals' faith had grown.

Developing Claims and Using Evidence

Try to determine if a news source is politically biased. Choose a source and review random political news stories found there. Highlight the passages that appear to be based on opinion rather than on fact. Use these highlighted passages to help support your argument of whether the news source is politically biased. What effect do you think this type of reporting can have on the public?

CHAPTER 4

Economics: The Numbers Behind It All

The media industry is vast and powerful, here and around the world. That means there's plenty of money flowing through it. The same goes for politics. Wherever there are people of power, money is always close by. What do the numbers say about the relationship between media and politics?

Money Helps, But So Does Coverage

In many countries, there is a limit to how much money can be given to a political candidate. This is true in the United States. This limit is set by a **campaign finance law**. It applies to both individuals and companies and prevents both from being able

An individual person in the United States can give up to $2,700 per election to a presidential candidate.

to influence a candidate. These laws are intended to keep political races fair, but there are ways around this law.

The media can help a candidate in ways that have nothing to do with money. In 2012, Mitt Romney ran against Barack Obama for president. During most of the campaign, there was plenty of positive and negative news coverage about both candidates. However, in the final week before the election, Obama received more favorable coverage in the news than Romney. According to a study, positive stories about Obama outnumbered negative ones by about 10 percent. In contrast, negative stories about Romney

Political campaign ads on TV are banned in Britain.

outnumbered positive ones by about 17 percent. The final week before an election is one of the most critical times in a campaign. Obama won.

The Business of Advertising

One of the main sources of income for any media organization is its **advertising revenue**. Since political advertisements are very important during any political race, most campaigns are willing to spend big.

Despite being ignored by the mainstream media during the 2008 presidential primary, Ron Paul raised about $4 million online.

Reports indicate that for every $5 spent on digital ads, $2 of that goes to social media sites, like Facebook.

Taking Informed Action

During any political campaign, you'll see both positive and negative news coverage on the candidates. Using the Internet and your local library, review the news coverage of candidates in past elections. Look at websites, magazines, newspapers, and television coverage from mainstream news sources. Compare your findings with news you find from **alternative news** sources, blogs, and podcasts. Determine which news sites provided a reasonable and balanced view of each candidate. Make a list of those that portrayed the candidates fairly. Was one source better than another?

In 2016, spending for political ads reached about $9.8 billion. And these ads are no longer simply on television or in print media, like newspapers and magazines. With the continual growth of online news—from social media to alternative news sites—a lot of money is going into online ads. In 2008, about $23 million was spent on online political ads. In 2016, that number skyrocketed to more than $1 billion! According to reports, almost half of the money spent on political online ads in 2016 went to social media sites, with Facebook being the top contender.

Communicating Conclusions

Before reading this book, did you know about the relationship between politics and the media? Now that you know more, why do you think it's important to learn about politics and how it's portrayed in the media? Do you feel you can trust it? Why or why not? Share your thoughts with friends and family. Use evidence you find in this book and the research you've done to support your argument.

Think About It

According to a study done after the 2016 presidential election, the media coverage of Donald Trump during his campaign was overwhelmingly negative. About 65 percent of all media stories portrayed him in a negative light. In addition, only about 11 percent of all news stories about Trump and his opponent, Hillary Clinton, focused on their political policies and proposals.

What do these statistics tell you about the state of the modern political media? What improvements do you feel need to be made? And if those improvements aren't made, what might be the consequences?

For More Information

Further Reading

Mahoney, Ellen Voelckers. *Nellie Bly and Investigative Journalism for Kids: Mighty Muckrakers from the Golden Age to Today, with 21 Activities.* Chicago: Chicago Review Press, 2015.

Mooney, Carla. *Asking Questions About How the News Is Created.* Ann Arbor, MI: Cherry Lake Publishing, 2016.

Weiss, Nancy E. *Asking Questions About Political Campaigns.* Ann Arbor, MI: Cherry Lake Publishing, 2016.

Websites

DOGO News—Kids News: Current Events
www.dogonews.com
Read about current events in the United States and around the world.

TIME for Kids—Government
www.timeforkids.com/g56/topics/government
Learn more about the United States government.

GLOSSARY

administration (ad-min-ih-STRAY-shuhn) the government of a particular president, including that president's cabinet and advisers

advertising revenue (AD-vur-tize-ing REV-uh-noo) money made by a media outlet from companies that want to promote products and services through them

alternative news (awl-TUR-nuh-tiv NOOZ) news that is separate and apart from mainstream news, reflecting less common views

bias (BYE-uhs) a tendency to favor or oppose a particular group or person

campaign finance law (kam-PAYN FYE-nans LAW) a law designed to keep wealthy donors from "buying" political candidates by donating more money than most other people could

conservative (kuhn-SUR-vuh-tiv) tending to value and maintain existing or traditional order; often referred to as the right or right wing

fake news (FEYK nooz) news that is published or broadcast with the intent to mislead people in order to destroy the reputation of a person, group of people, or organization

free speech (FREE SPEECH) the right to speak, write, or otherwise communicate freely about what is on your mind

groupthink (GROOP-thingk) a pattern of thought that happens when pressure to agree within a group results in everyone thinking the same way about an issue, situation, or decision

journalists (JUR-nuh-lists) people who find and report on stories that are newsworthy

liberal (LIB-ur-uhl) in favor of political progress; often referred to as the left or left wing

mainstream news (MAYN-streem NOOZ) refers to the various large and popular mass news media

media (ME-dee-uh) a method of communication between people, such as a newspaper

objective (uhb-JEK-tiv) reporting a news story in a way that is not affected by the journalist's personal views

polarization (poh-lur-ih-ZAY-shun) a division between groups of people with differing viewpoints

politics (pol-uh-TIKS) the activities and discussions involved in governing a country, state, or city, including the activities of those who serve in government

printing press (PRINT-ing PRES) a device designed to print ink onto paper in large quantities

watchdog (WAHCH-dawg) a person or organization that monitors news sites and guards them against dishonesty

INDEX